HOW THINGS WORK!

SIMPLE MECHANISMS

ADE DEANE-PRATT

WAYLAND

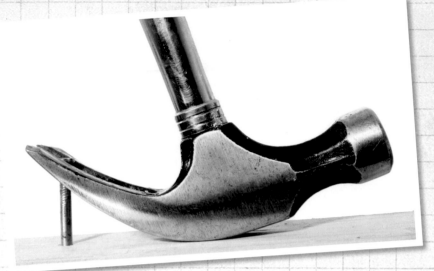

Published in 2013 by Wayland

Copyright © Wayland 2013

Wayland
338 Euston Road
London NW1 3BH

Wayland Australia
Level 17/207 Kent Street
Sydney NSW 2000

Editor: Julia Adams

Pro...
Edit... Rob Colson and Jennifer ...derson
Con...
Step... ...Watson
Des...

Brit...
Dea...
1.
I.
6...

ISBN 978 0 7502 7176 9

Printed in China

Wayland is a division of Hachette Children's Books,
an Hachette UK company.
www.hachette.co.uk

Picture credits

The publisher would would like to thank the following for
their kind permission to reproduce their photographs:
key: (t) top; (c) centre; (b) bottom; (l) left; (r) right
1 Intst/Dreamstime.com; 2 Baronuk/Dreamstime.com;
4 Sergej Razvodovskij/Dreamstime.com; 5 Igor Strukov/
Dreamstime.com; 7 (t) Baronuk/Dreamstime.com,
(c) Nicky Linzey/Dreamstime.com, (b) Andi Berger/
Dreamstime.com; 9 (t) Juriah Mosin/Dreamstime.com,
(c) Phartisan/Dreamstime.com, (b) Arenacreative/
Dreamstime.com; 11 (t) Rob Cruse/iStock, (bl)
Chrisp543/Dreamstime.com, (br) wiktor bubniak/i-Stock;
12 Dreamstime.com; 13 (t) US Navy, (c) Alexander
Klimenko/Dreamstime.com, (b) Evgeniy Gritsun/
Dreamstime.com; 14 Photka/Dreamstime.com; 15 (tr)
Scanrail/Dreamstime.com, (tl) Jkitan/Dreamstime.com,
(c) Homydesign/Dreamstime.com, (b) Bjorn Heller/
Dreamstime.com; 17 (t) Intst/Dreamstime.com, (c)
Andrey Yakovlev/ Dreamstime.com, (b) Paulbroad/
Dreamstime.com; 19 (t) Dario Sabljak/ shutterstock.
com; 19 (b) Wayland; 20 (t) Ahmet Ihsan Ariturk/
Dreamstime.com, (bl) Wikipedia Commons, (br)
Paparico/Dreamstime.com

Disclaimer

CONTENTS

MAKING WORK EASIER

A mechanism is a mechanical device that transmits force from one place to another. These mechanisms can combine to make machines. Machines can be simple, such as a screw, or complex, such as cars.

WHY DO WE NEED MACHINES?

Machines make a job easier to do. Some machines, such as bicycles, speed up movement. Other machines, such as ramps, slow down movement. We can also use machines to stop an object from moving. We rely on machines for almost everything we do.

A knife is an example of a simple machine called a wedge. It is used to cut or separate things, such as fruit and vegetables.

THE SIMPLE MACHINES

A specific group of six mechanisms is called the 'simple machines'. These are levers, wheels, pulleys, ramps, wedges and screws. This book looks at these simple machines and other mechanisms. The project pages will show you that by combining some of them, you will be able to make machines, such as a cardboard van, moving monster head, a balance and a well.

A crane combines levers, pulleys and wheels to produce a machine that can lift heavy objects and move them from one place to another.

LIFTING IT UP

A simple machine called a lever allows you to lift a heavy load. Levers can also be used to move a light load over a long distance.

HOW DOES IT WORK?

Levers are made of two parts: the arm and the pivot. The arm carries the load and moves by turning around the pivot. Levers move a load when a force, or effort, is applied to the arm. The further away from the pivot you apply the effort, the less the effort has to be to move the load. There are three different types, or classes, of lever, depending on where the pivot and the load are placed, and where the effort is applied.

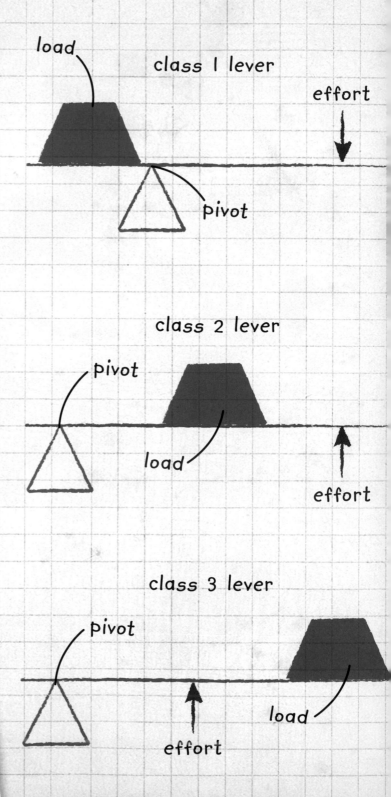

load
class 1 lever
effort
pivot

class 2 lever
pivot
load
effort

class 3 lever
pivot
load
effort

Try it !

Balance a stiff ruler across a pencil that is on a table. Place a stack of four identical coins on the ruler to one side of the pencil, about half way between the pencil and the end of the ruler. Now stack coins on the other side of the pencil, right at the end of the ruler. How many coins balance the ruler?

This hammer is used as a class 1 lever. The pivot is between the load and the effort. The effort applied on the handle of the hammer is transferred to its head, which pulls out the nail.

load

effort

pivot

LEVERS IN ACTION

Look around you and see how many levers you can find. You may find them in surprising places: the ring pull on a can of fizzy drink is an example of a lever. The human body has many levers, too, such as arms and legs. These use joints, or pivots, such as the elbow, to make us move or lift things.

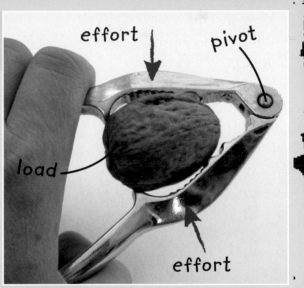

Nutcrackers are made up of two class 2 levers. The load and the effort are on the same side of the pivot. The nut is the load. It is placed close to the pivot, where the two arms are joined. The effort is the hand pressing the arms together at the other end.

effort

pivot

load

effort

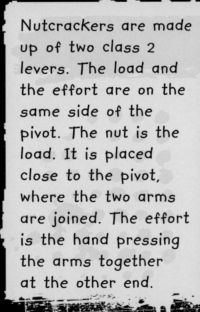

load

effort

pivot

The human arm is a class 3 lever. The elbow is the pivot and the load is whatever you are holding. The effort is applied between the load and the elbow to lift the load.

USING RAMPS

A ramp is a flat, sloping surface. It is designed to make it easier and safer to raise and lower objects slowly.

HOW DOES IT WORK?

It is easier to raise an object by pushing it up the slope of a ramp than by trying to lift it. You need less effort to move the object up, but you have to push it further. The shallower the ramp, the less effort you need to use, but the farther you have to push the object. Ramps can also be used to move things safely and more easily from a high place to a lower one by slowing down the downwards movement.

distance travelled up ramp

vertical distance

steep ramp

distance travelled up ramp

shallow ramp

RAMPS IN ACTION

Some ramps, for example slides in amusement parks, are used only for going downwards. Others, such as the ramp on a breakdown lorry or a wheelchair access ramp, are used to move objects both up and down.

A broken-down car is dragged up onto the breakdown truck using a ramp. The car can also be safely lowered using the same ramp.

Ramps are used as slides. They need to be steep enough to make the ride exciting but slope gently enough to be safe.

Skateboarders go up and down the ramps of a halfpipe to build the height needed to do aerial tricks.

WEDGES AT WORK

When you cut something with a knife, you are using a wedge. Wedges are v-shaped blocks used to cut or separate objects. They can also be used to hold things in place.

HOW DOES IT WORK?

A wedge changes the direction of a force. When you push on the flat end of a wedge, the downward force produces other forces that are perpendicular to the sloping sides. The blade of a knife is wedge-shaped. When you cut up food, you push down on the blade. The wedge shape of the blade turns some of the downwards force into sideways force that pushes the sides of the food apart.

A short, thick wedge will split things apart faster but will need more force. A long, thin wedge is easier to drive in, but will take longer to split an object.

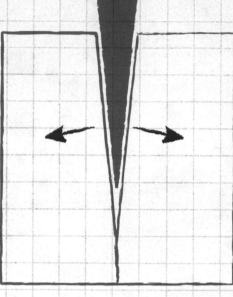

force

long, thin wedge

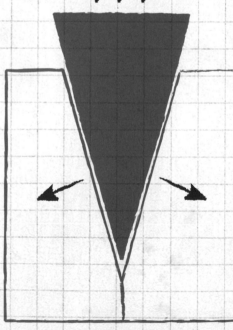

force

short, thick wedge

Try it !

Take a very blunt pencil and try to push it into an eraser. Now sharpen the pencil to a point and then push it into the eraser again. Which was easier to push in – the blunt pencil or the sharp one?

A wedge can act as a door stop by turning the force of the door pushing against it into a force that pushes back up at the door and down against the floor, holding the door in place.

WEDGES IN ACTION

Door-stops are wedges that hold objects in place. Nails, axes, the prongs on a fork and knives are all wedges that cut or separate objects. Sharp knives are easier to use because the wedge on the blade is longer and thinner than the wedge on a blunt knife.

The head of an axe is heavy and has a sharp wedge-shaped blade. Its weight helps to create enough force to chop wood.

Sculptors use wedge-shaped chisels to chip away at hard materials such as marble. The sculptor bangs the blunt end of the chisel with a hammer, and the sharp end cuts into the marble.

ScRewIng iT iN

Many everyday objects are held together by screws. Screws are simple machines that can change a turning force into forwards movement.

HOW DOES IT WORK?

Screws change turning motion into movement in a straight line. They can also work the other way round to change forwards motion into a turning force. A screw is a ramp wrapped around a central rod. The ramp forms a ridge, called a thread. As a screw turns, the thread grips the surface it is moving into. This pulls the screw and the surface together. The turning motion is provided by an outside force, for example, from a screwdriver.

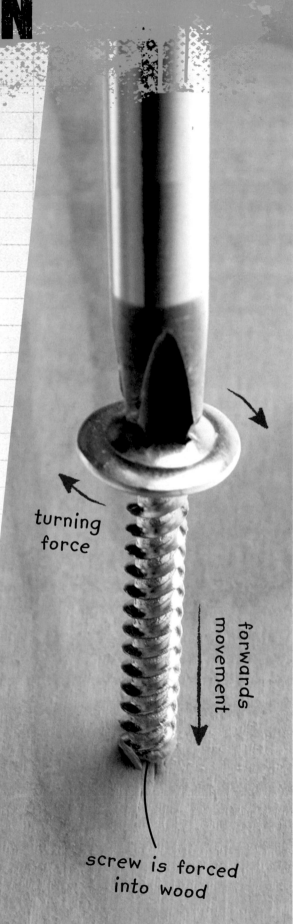

turning force

forwards movement

screw is forced into wood

Try it !

Take a screw and hold it against a piece of scrap wood. Push against the end of the screw and try to force it into the wood. Now use a screwdriver to turn in the screw. The combination of the pushing and turning of the screwdriver allows you to twist the screw into the wood.

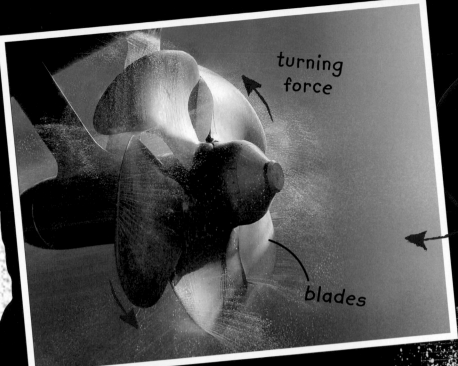

turning force

blades

The blades of a propeller are twisted like the thread of a screw. As the propeller turns, it pushes the water backwards and the boat forwards.

SCREWS IN ACTION

Everyday examples of screws include jam jar lids, ships' propellers and corkscrews. Screws can hold things together, such as the different parts of a chair or table. Screws can also move things, such as the cork out of a bottle.

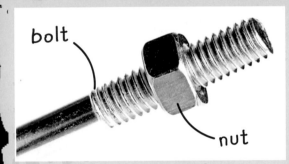

bolt

nut

A bolt is a type of screw that turns inside a nut to assemble things. The nut has a matching thread that grips onto the thread of the bolt, moving the nut along the bolt as it turns.

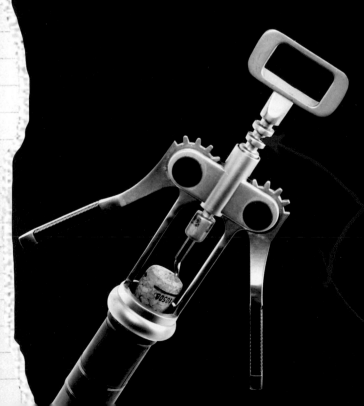

Turning the thread of a corkscrew into the cork gives enough grip to pull out the cork. Wing corkscrews also use levers to help pull out the cork.

rOUND AND rOUND

Cars, trucks, motorbikes and bicycles all have wheels that move an object from one place to another. A wheel is circular and turns around a rod in its centre, called an axle.

HOW DOES IT WORK?

Wheels reduce the amount of force needed to move an object along the ground compared to simply pushing it along. They can be solid or they can have spokes. Wheels with spokes are lighter than solid wheels so they need less effort to move, making it easier for a cyclist to pedal. The tyres around the wheel have tread to give them a better grip on the road.

distance travelled by one rotation

spokes

rim

axle

tyre

Try it !

Tie some string tightly around a book. Drag the book across a table. Now have another go, but this time, start with the book on top of some pencils with rounded sides. Which way is easier?

WHEELS IN ACTION

While wheels are found on most vehicles, they can also be added to everyday objects, such as luggage or furniture, to make it easier to move them from place to place.

Ball bearings are small balls placed between the wheels inside machines such as skateboards. Like wheels, the balls turn to make the machine move more smoothly.

ball bearing

Racing bicycles have large wheels that move the cyclist a long distance with each turn. This helps the cyclist reach high speeds. BMX bicycles have smaller wheels as the cyclist needs to have more control over his bike to do tricks.

Tractors have wide wheels. This means that a larger area of the tyre touches the ground at any one time. This stops the tractor sinking in soft ground.

CHANGING GEARS

Gears are wheels with teeth around their rims. The wheels spin around and turn other gears as they move. Gears can change the speed or direction of a turning motion or keep two parts of a machine working in time with each other.

HOW DOES IT WORK?

Gears work in groups of two or more. As one gear turns, its teeth lock in between the teeth of another gear. Force is transferred from the first gear to the second. The second gear turns in the opposite direction to the first. Systems of gears can change a force by either increasing or decreasing the speed of rotation. A small gear attached to a large gear will rotate more quickly than the large gear. You can speed up rotation by applying force to the large gear, or slow it down by applying force to the small one.

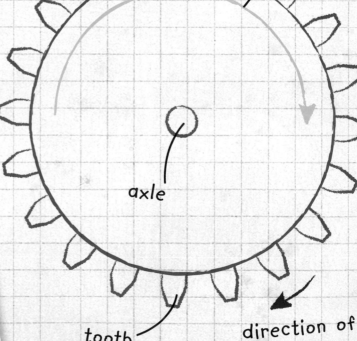

direction of rotation (anti-clockwise)

the small gear makes one rotation for every half rotation of the large gear

axle

tooth

direction of rotation (clockwise)

Try it !

Look at the gears on a bicycle. The gears at the front are powered by the pedals. They are attached to the gears on the back wheel by the chain. When you cycle, change to a lower gear and pedal, is it easier to pedal or do you need to pedal harder to move?

The two hands of a clock are each connected to a set of gears. The gears change the speed of the clock's motor to move the hands at the right speed.

GEARS IN ACTION

Gears are used in many machines, from clocks to bicycles and from sewing machines to trains. The motor of a sewing machine operates gears, which move the needle up and down to complete a stitch.

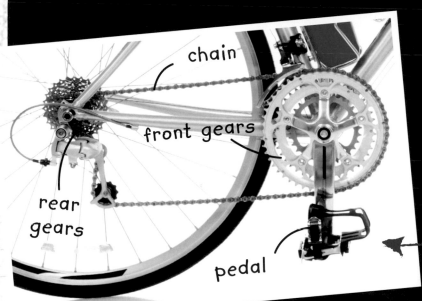

chain

front gears

rear gears

pedal

On a bicycle's rear wheel, the larger cogs are the lower gears. They are easier to turn and are used to cycle uphill. The smaller cogs are the higher gears. They are harder to turn and are used to cycle at high speeds.

The gearbox inside a car has several gears. They move the car forwards at different speeds. Cars also have a reverse gear to move them backwards.

PULLEY POWER

Cranes, flagpoles and sailing boats all use pulleys. Pulleys combine wheels with a rope or belt to lift or pull objects.

HOW DOES IT WORK?

A rope moves around the wheel of a pulley to change the direction of a force. For example, you can use a pulley to lift an object upwards by attaching one end to the object and pulling down on the other end. Several pulleys can be used together to make work easier. The more pulleys you use, the greater the distance you need to pull down the rope to lift the load, but the less effort you need to use.

single fixed pulley

double pulley

effort

effort

load

load

a second pulley decreases the effort needed to move an object

Try it !

Tie one end of a piece of string to a shoe – this is your load. Loop the string around a cotton reel. Use one hand to lift the cotton reel into the air, and pull down on the loose end of the string with your other hand. As you pull down, what happens to the load?

Window cleaners move up and down outside high-rise buildings in a special gondola attached to pulleys.

PULLEYS IN ACTION

Simple pulleys can be used on their own, for example on a flagpole. By pulling down on the rope, the flag is hoisted to the top of the flagpole. Pulleys can also be combined with other simple or more complex machines to do more difficult tasks, for example in sailing boats.

Sailors on yachts use pulleys to move the sails into different positions so that they catch the wind and move the yacht.

USING LIQUID AND GAS

Gases and liquids can be used to move objects. Using gases is called 'pneumatics', while using liquids is called 'hydraulics'.

HOW DOES IT WORK?

When gas or liquid is put inside two containers that are connected by a tube, they can pass on forces. Pushing down on a rod, or piston, in one of the containers squeezes the gas or liquid along the tube to the other container. Then the gas or liquid pushes on the piston attached to the other container.

Pistons can be used to change the size of a force. If you push down on a small piston, the force will be passed on to the big piston by the liquid. There will be a bigger force on the large piston, but it will not move as far as the small piston did.

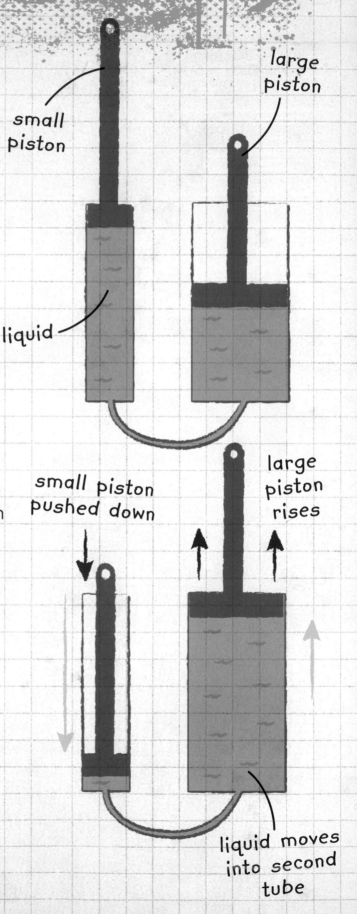

small piston

large piston

liquid

small piston pushed down

large piston rises

liquid moves into second tube

Try it !

Lay a paper bag flat on a table with a book on top of it. Blow into the bag and watch it fill up and lift the book. How many books can you lift?

On a large tipper truck, the hydraulic piston pushes up the back of the truck to dump the load.

hydraulic piston

HYDRAULICS AND PNEUMATICS IN ACTION

Hydraulics are used in machines such as diggers, bulldozers and fork-lift trucks, which lift heavy weights. They are also used in car brakes. Pneumatics are used in the brakes of trains and large trucks, and to power the drills that are used to dig up roads.

The arm of this toy digger uses hydraulics. Its pistons move in and out to move the arm up and down and forward and back, enabling the bucket to scoop up things.

A pneumatic drill is powered by rapid blasts of air. Each blast drives the drill bit down into the road.

Make a balance

Weigh anything from sugar to shoes with this balance! You will need an adult's help to drill the holes.

what you need

- ruler
- pencil
- piece of wood 50 cm (20 in) long, 4 cm wide, 1cm (½ in) thick
- drill and drill bit of equal size to the wing nut
- piece of wood 50 cm (20 in) long, 4 cm (1½ in) wide and 4 cm (1½ in) thick
- piece of wood 50 cm (20 in) long, 20 cm (8 in) wide and 1 cm (½ in) thick
- two shelf brackets
- screws to fit the brackets
- screwdriver
- wing nut
- string
- bag of sugar
- spring balance

1 To make the arm of the balance, measure out and mark five holes, 10 cm (4 in) apart, along the first piece of wood. Ask an adult to drill holes on your marks. Drill a hole 5 cm (2 in) from one end of the second piece of wood to form the upright.

2 The third piece of wood forms the base. Use the screwdriver and screws to attach the brackets and fix the upright to the base. Make sure that the hole you drilled in the upright in step 1 is facing the long edge of the base.

3 Line up the hole in the middle of the arm with the hole at the top of the upright. Fix the arm to the upright with the wing nut. Make sure that the arm can swing freely.

22

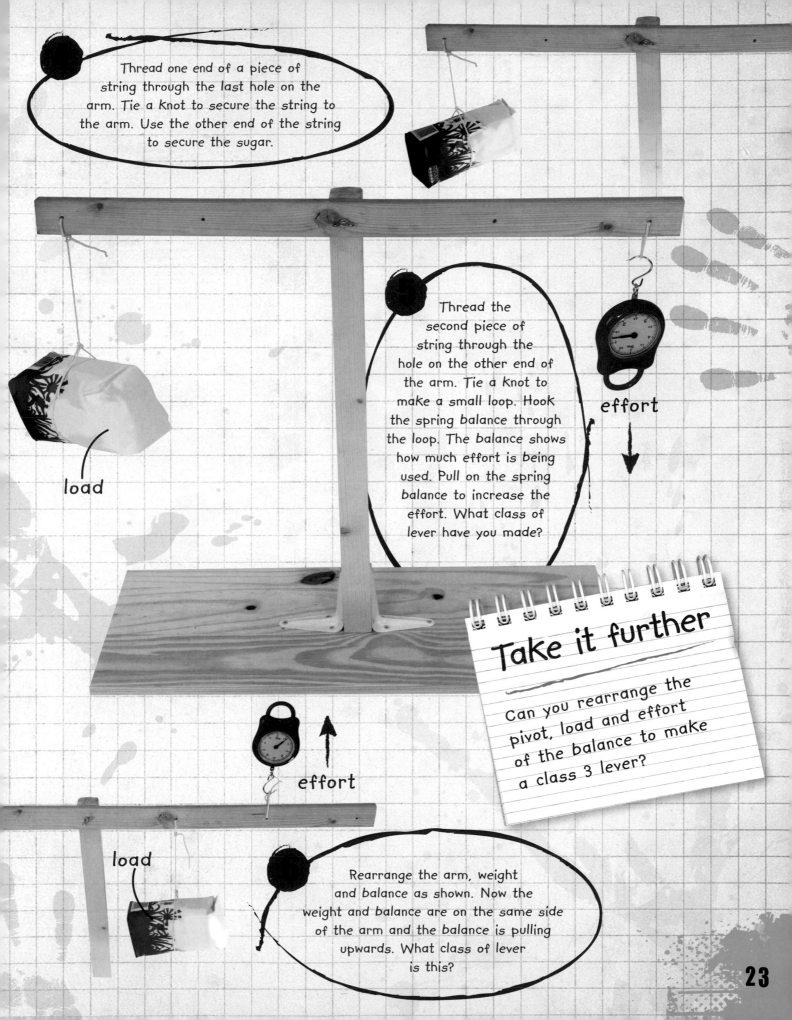

Thread one end of a piece of string through the last hole on the arm. Tie a knot to secure the string to the arm. Use the other end of the string to secure the sugar.

load

Thread the second piece of string through the hole on the other end of the arm. Tie a knot to make a small loop. Hook the spring balance through the loop. The balance shows how much effort is being used. Pull on the spring balance to increase the effort. What class of lever have you made?

effort

Take it further

Can you rearrange the pivot, load and effort of the balance to make a class 3 lever?

effort

load

Rearrange the arm, weight and balance as shown. Now the weight and balance are on the same side of the arm and the balance is pulling upwards. What class of lever is this?

Make a cardboard van

This van uses a combination of machines, from levers to wheels, to make it move.

what you need

- cardboard box about 40 cm (16 in) long, 30 cm (12 in) wide and 30 cm (12 in) high
- scissors
- paint and brushes
- PVA glue
- drinking straws
- sticky tape
- 3 pieces of garden cane about 30 cm (12 in) long
- four round sponges

1 To make the van's body, cut all the flaps off the cardboard box. Keep the flaps for later use. Cut out an arch on either side of the box big enough to fit the round sponges. They need to be exactly opposite each other. Paint the box to decorate your van.

glue here · width of van · hole

2 Take one of the flaps cut from the box, and fold it at both ends so that it is as long as the width of the van. This is the axle mounting point. Make a hole in the centre of the axle mounting point. Glue the axle mounting point to the inside of the body of the van.

20 cm (8 in)

20 cm (8 in)

3 Tape two straws together in a T-shape to make the steering column and axle. Push a piece of garden cane into the straws to extend the T to 30 cm (12 in) long. Tape them securely.

steering column

axle

4 Make a hole in the roof of the van 10 cm (4 in) from the front and 15 cm (6 in) from the edge. Push the steering column through the hole in the axle mounting point and up through the top of the body.

5 To make the wheels, cut out four circles of card left over from the box. They need to be a smaller than the round sponges. Glue a circle to each sponge. For the front wheels, push a piece of garden cane into the back of one wheel.

6 Thread the cane through the T part of the axle made in step 3. Push another sponge onto the other end of the cane for the second front wheel.

7 Use the pencil to make a hole 8 cm (3 in) from the back of the van and 3 cm (1 in) from the bottom edge on either side of the van. Push a piece of garden cane into the back of one wheel, then thread the cane through the holes. Attach the remaining sponge to complete the last wheel.

Take it further

What happens if you push the van backwards and turn the steering wheel? Does the van follow the same path?

8 Cut a circle of card 10 cm (4 in) in diameter to make the steering wheel. Use paint to decorate it. Glue the steering wheel to the top of the steering column. Move the van forward and turn the steering wheel. When you turn the steering wheel, the axle turns, too. The van will follow the wheels and turn a corner.

Make a well

Wells are used to draw water to the surface from underground. This well uses a pulley to move the bucket.

what you need

- scissors
- plastic cup
- ball of string
- sticky tape
- cotton reel
- A4-size stiff card
- piece of plain white paper
- PVA glue
- paints and paintbrush
- garden cane 30 cm (12 in) long
- empty paint pot
- modelling clay
- two bendy drinking straws

1 Start by making the bucket's handle. Use the scissors to make two small holes in either side of the top of the cup. Thread a piece of string 15 cm (6 in) long through both holes. Tie knots at each end to keep the string in place.

sticky tape

2 Tie a 1-m (40-in) piece of string to the middle of the handle. Tape the other end of the string to the cotton reel and wind it round the reel.

3 Cut two narrow 5-cm (2-in) wide strips from the stiff card. Make a hole into each strip 5 cm (2 in) from one end. These will be the uprights of your well.

4 Glue white paper around the paint pot to cover it, then paint the pot and the uprights to decorate them.

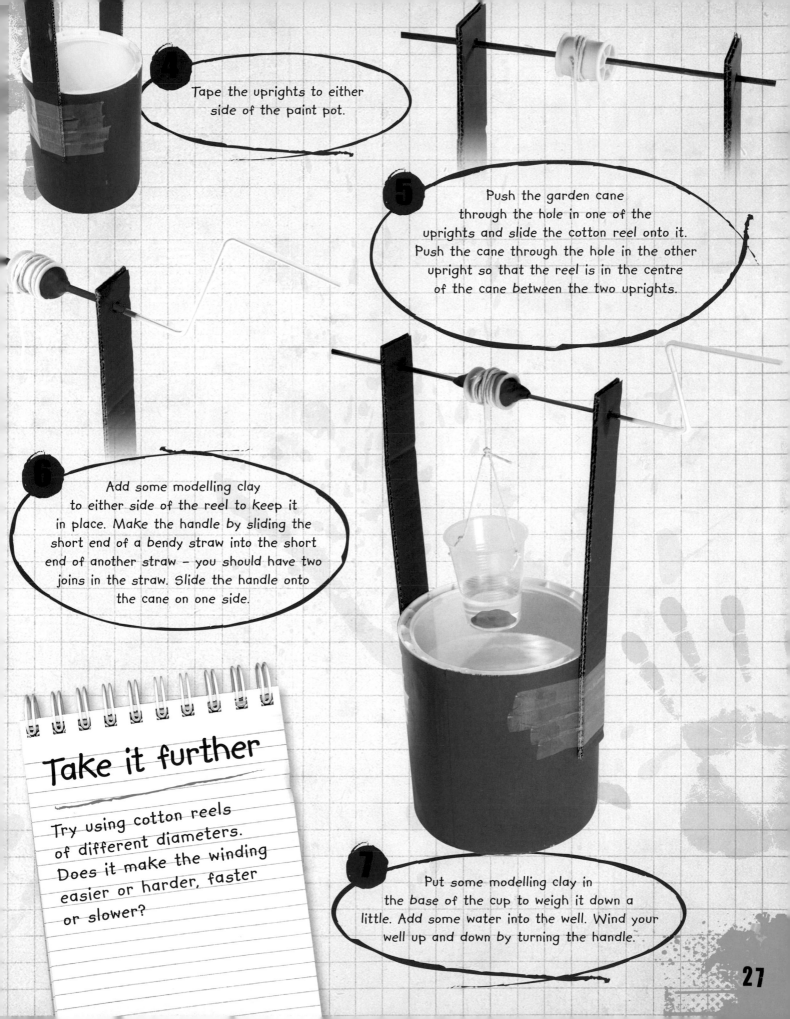

4 Tape the uprights to either side of the paint pot.

5 Push the garden cane through the hole in one of the uprights and slide the cotton reel onto it. Push the cane through the hole in the other upright so that the reel is in the centre of the cane between the two uprights.

6 Add some modelling clay to either side of the reel to keep it in place. Make the handle by sliding the short end of a bendy straw into the short end of another straw – you should have two joins in the straw. Slide the handle onto the cane on one side.

Take it further

Try using cotton reels of different diameters. Does it make the winding easier or harder, faster or slower?

7 Put some modelling clay in the base of the cup to weigh it down a little. Add some water into the well. Wind your well up and down by turning the handle.

Make a monster's head

Snap this monster's pneumatic jaws open and shut to give someone a fright!

what you need

- large piece of thick card
- scissors
- paint and paintbrushes
- hole punch
- paper fastener
- sticky tape
- wooden stick
- two syringes
- 20 cm (8 in) long piece of 5-mm (0.2-in) tubing

1 Draw a monster's head on the card in two parts – the upper jaw and the lower jaw. Give your monster big, sharp teeth. Cut out the two pieces and decorate them.

2 Use a hole punch to make a hole at the back of each jaw. Attach them to each other using the paper fastener. Make sure that the jaws can move freely.

paper fastener

sticky tape

3 Tape the wooden stick to the upper jaw so that it is firmly held in place.

4 Tape the body of one syringe to the back of the lower jaw. Tape the top of its plunger to the upper jaw.

plunger

5 Keeping the plunger out of the second syringe, link the two syringes with the tubing. Insert the plunger into the second syringe.

Take it further

• You have made pneumatic jaws that are powered by air. How would you change them to make hydraulic jaws powered by liquid?

• What other power sources could be used to move the jaws? Which do you think would work best?

6 Hold the monster's head by the wooden stick in one hand and the free syringe in the other. Push on the free syringe and watch your monster open its mouth!

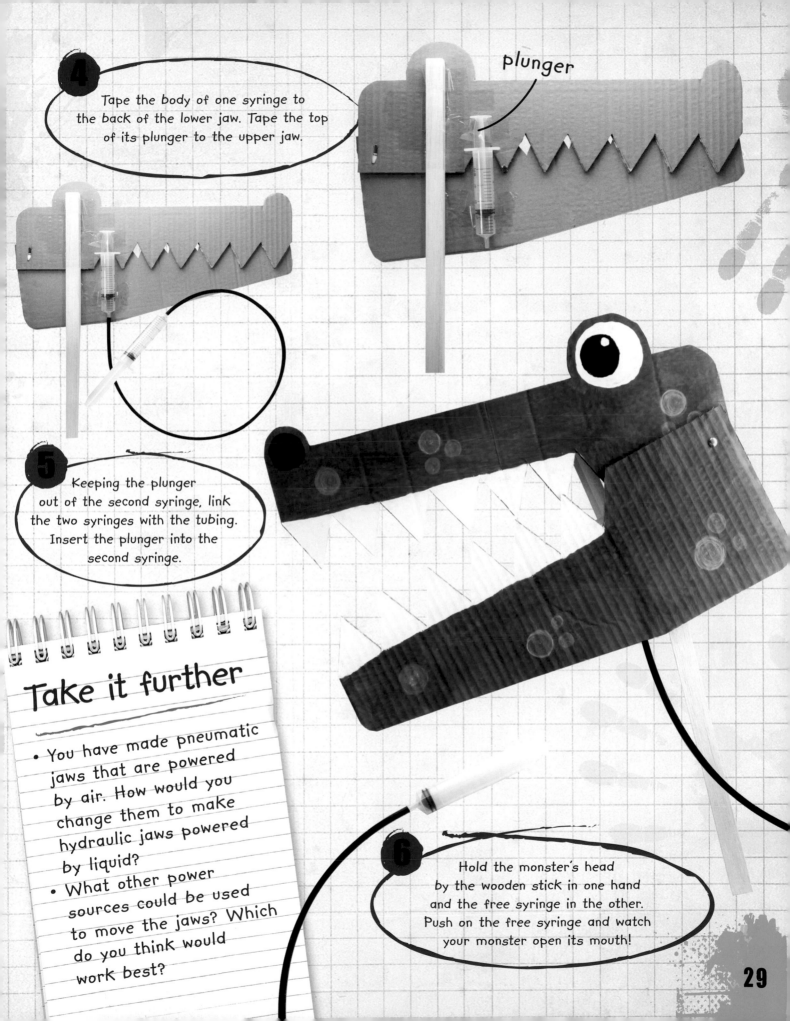

GLOSSARY

axle
The bar or shaft on which a wheel rotates, or turns around.

ball bearings
Metal balls arranged in a ring to make parts of a machine, such as wheels, move more easily.

blade
The sharp, wedge-shaped part of tools such as knives and axes, which are used to cut objects.

cogs
The tooth-like parts found around the edge of a wheel. Cogs are part of a system of gears.

effort
The force needed to move an object.

force
Something that acts to change the speed or direction of movement of an object, or its shape.

friction
The resistance to movement that occurs when two objects are in contact.

gears
Wheels with teeth around their edges that spin and turn around other gears as they move.

gondola
A large hanging basket in which people sit or travel.

hydraulics
Using water or other liquids to make an object move.

lever
A simple machine used to lift or move a heavy load.

perpendicular
When something is at 90 degrees, or a right angle, to another object.

piston
A solid cylinder or disc that fits into a hollow tube and moves backwards and forwards.

pivot
A fixed point that supports something that turns or balances.

pneumatics
Using gases, such as air, to make an object move.

propeller
A device made of a series of twisted blades on a shaft that turn around.

pulley
A simple machine, with a rope that goes over a wheel, which is used to lift or move heavy objects.

ramp
A flat, sloping surface used to move an object upwards or downwards.

rotation
When something turns around completely.

spokes
The rods that join the edge of a wheel to its centre to give the wheel its strength.

thread
A continuous raised line, such as the one that goes around the outside of a screw or bolt, or the inside of a hole.

wedge
A v-shaped block used to cut or separate things or to hold things in place.

TOPIC WEB

Use this topic web to discover themes and ideas in subjects that are related to simple mechanisms.

Design and technology
Use a combination of simple machines to invent a tool or machine for the construction industry. What materials would you use? Draw labelled diagrams to illustrate your invention.

Science
The body is a machine! Find out the joints in the human body and how they act as levers. You may want to illustrate your findings.

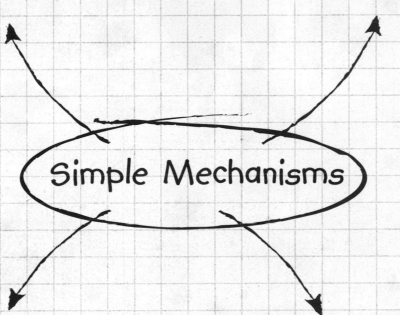

Simple Mechanisms

Art
Collect a range of simple machines, such as nuts, bolts, nails and cogs, to make a sculpture of a larger machine.

History
Find out about machines in the Victorian age. What simple machines did they use to invent larger, more complex machines.